THE OTHER SIDE OF GRIEF

BOUNCING BACK FROM GRIEF INTO AN ABUNDANT LIFE

A 30-DAY DEVOTIONAL TO INSPIRE YOU INTO A LIFE OF EVERLASTING JOY

Apostle L'Tanya C. Perry, MDIV.

TAP
TRAINING WITH
APOSTLE PERRY

Paperback ISBN: 978-1-957052-86-1
Hardcover- ISBN: 978-1-957052-84-7
Ebook-ISBN: 978-1-957052-83-0

Printed in the United States of America.

TAP Press

TAP Press Publishing
PO BOX 561
Granite Falls, NC 28630

Acknowledgements

I dedicate this book to God Almighty, who never left me during my grieving. Your voice was so clear and frequent in so many ways, through Your Word, dreams, visions, and people around me. You answered all my questions sometimes instantly and in bits according to Your will to restore comfort to my heart. It's amazing how Your Truth brings healing.

I also dedicate this book to my Mom, who has gone to be with the Lord. I miss you so much. You trained me to stand in any situation and keep trusting God as my source. You demonstrated how to trust God in everything. Grandma Louise McCorkle would say, "Keep God first in everything you do!" I hear her voice saying that to me daily.

I also dedicate this book to my husband, Kelvin Perry, Sr.—no words to express my gratitude for your comfort during my grieving stages. We had a tough year with death hitting our family every couple of months in 2021. We both grieved and still had to work while taking short pauses between moving our son out to go off to college, traveling with him to his ball games, Alexus moving into her first new home, and learning to be empty nesters, Oooo... I forgot our grand-dog, Blue, staying here and there. So much happened in one year, and God still held us up. Thank you, Honey! I love you!

How can I forget my children, Alexus and KJ, and my niece, Maya? You have a wonderful grandmother. I said *have* because I'm certain she has eternal life in Heaven even though her natural body is no longer with us. I know that is challenging; however, Mom taught us so much. She spent a lot of time with you. Don't forget all she shared with you. She wants you to live a Godly life and succeed in making good decisions. Be in healthy relationships that bring joy. Don't let the devil use you; else you may grieve for eternity.

Finally, I dedicate this book to New Beginnings Worship Center Citizens. Thank you for being so patient with me during my time of mourning. You know how important my mom was to me and how she played a vital role in plowing the work at the church. You guys were flexible through in-person and virtual services. We had many challenges for those who left the ministry, school issues causing us only to have virtual services, and many other things. But you remained faithful. May God honor our labor of love. He told us, "All things work together for the good for those who love the Lord and called to His purpose." (Romans 8:28) God continues to confirm and speak to us. We shall continue this eternal race with our Helper!

And to you holding this book, Yes, you! Read, be encouraged! I pray that you find hope in this grieving season. I believe that every line in this book will resonate with joy and restoration to your heart. I pray you will dream again and encounter God in a new light. Thank you for choosing this unique path of truth.

Table Of Contents

Day 1

WHEN WORDS AREN'T ENOUGH

Scriptural Text: *A soft answer turns away wrath, but a harsh word stirs up anger.*

Proverbs 15:1 (ESV)

Inspiring Commentary

Whenever there's grief, majority of the time death has occurred. But death doesn't only affect the deceased. It casts it's depressing shadows on the bereaved, threatening to strangle the remaining life. People who lose their loved ones claim that something dies in them.

Therefore, when visitors come to comfort someone grieving, they shouldn't come with words of consolation alone. Mere words can't overcome death; only life can. Those who have grieved know that the words of comfort are thoughtful and kind. However, they can't pull the bereaved out of the swamp of grief.

Everyone who has lost their loved one needs someone, not something. He alone can utter words that give life or turn ordinary words into estuaries of living water to refresh the soul. His name is the Holy Spirit. (John 6:63 [AMPC]) says, *"It is the Spirit Who gives life [He is the Life-giver]; the flesh conveys no benefit whatever [there is no profit in it]. The words (truths) that I have been speaking to you are Spirit and life."*

The Holy Spirit has the power to take you past the pain and effects of your loss. Losing someone is an experience, so the Holy Spirit helps you by bringing you into a different experience. He makes the love of God real to you and launches you into a new dimension of life. As death attempts to corrupt your dreams and even the desire to live, He introduces the abundant life of Christ and flushes out the power of death.

I share in my book, *The Other Side of Grief* that, "It's the Holy Spirit's specialty to comfort those who grieve. He knows the vacuum your loss has created and how to fill it back up. If you're a believer, the Holy Spirit stepped into your life when you said yes to Jesus.

Here are some specific works of the Holy Spirit and how they apply to your broken heart. (John 16:13-15 [NKJV]) says, "*However, when He, the Spirit of truth, has come, He will guide you into all truth; for He will not speak on His own authority, but whatever He hears He will speak; and He will tell you things to come. He will glorify Me, for He will take of what is Mine and declare it to you. All things that the Father has are Mine. Therefore, I said that He will take of Mine and declare it to you.*" He will speak to guide you out of the swamp of grief. He will show you the glorious future God has planned for you. He's the Spirit that gives life, so He'll reveal that there are still many victories and celebrations ahead. Also, He'll teach your heart to trust, love, and hope again."[1]

How do you get the Holy Spirit to do all these things? By asking Him. The Holy Spirit won't come on the scene until you give the invitation. Jesus calls Him your Helper, so you must tell Him you need His help.

Call to Action

- What part of your life do you need the Holy Spirit to help you at this time?

____

____

____

____

Prayers

Father, in the name of Jesus, I thank You for this truth of Your Word to me today. I pray that You surround me with the right words that will take away my pain at this time. I pray that the Holy Spirit will guide my thoughts and my heart out of the swamp of grief into the fullness of joy in Christ. In Jesus' name. Amen.

Reflection

Day 2

LIFE CAN BE BEAUTIFUL AGAIN

Scriptural Text: *"At least there is hope for a tree: If it is cut down, it will sprout again, and its new shoots will not fail. Its roots may grow old in the ground and its stump die in the soil, yet at the scent of water it will bud and put forth shoots like a plant."*

Job 14:7-9 (KJV)

Inspiring Commentary

Have you ever been in a dare condition that seemed impossible to get out of? I've been there. In an impossible situation, the natural thing to do is doubt there's a way out. It seemed impossible when an angel appeared to Mary and shared God's will for her. She could only ask, "How shall these things be?" Although Mary didn't doubt God's ability, her mind couldn't fathom that such a thing was possible--how can a virgin give birth?

Now, to a grieving person, the possibility of getting over the loss is as incredulous as a virgin giving birth. Again, "How shall these things be?" comes up. But the answer is the same as the one Mary received. The Holy Spirit.

Whenever there's a need for someone to go beyond the limitations of the natural, the only sufficient transport system is the Holy Spirit. The truth is, the possibilities He administers are supposed to be part of the normal Christian life. It shouldn't be strange to a believer that the Holy Spirit can give joy where there's pain and hope where there's despair.

I shared these thoughts in my book, *The Other Side of Grief* that, "The death of a loved one often robs life of its beauty. The Holy Spirit specializes in restoring that beauty. If you're still wondering "How," here's an amazing answer. The Holy Spirit doesn't make you forget that bond or reduce that person's value to you. Of course not. He introduces another bond—His bond with you. He makes your relationship with the Father, the Lord Jesus, and Himself real to you. Just as you were blessed by those you lost, you ought to be blessed by God's presence. So the Holy Spirit fills your life through fellowship.

Now, when anyone suffers a loss, it can be said that they have experienced great desolation. You're like a city that got abandoned or deserted. There's no more laughter, hope, and joy. The energy you once had is gone, and the things that pleased you have lost their appeal. Life seems desolate. But not to worry. This is the expertise of the Holy Spirit. He can bring transformation to the most hopeless situation.

Indeed, when a city is desolate because it has been raided or abandoned, the walls are broken down and the structures destroyed. It doesn't need one or two fixes. It needs to be rebuilt. The ideal word is transformation. And that's what the Holy Spirit brings into your life."[2]

Many Christians don't experience the reality of the Holy Spirit's help. Why? Because they've not learned to fellowship with Him. This simply means to establish and maintain intimacy with Him. Without fellowship, you can't access the many possibilities locked up in your relationship with God.

Call To Action

- What are the impossibilities around your life that your loss has caused?

___

___

- What are the possibilities you have now discovered in Christ regarding your loss?

Prayer

Father, in the name of Jesus, I thank You for the light of Your work shining on my heart today. I know it seems impossible to bounce back from this situation into the fullness of life again, but now I see the light. I know that all things are possible with You, so I pray that You help me. Show me and teach me Your way out of this misery into peace again. Let my joy sprout again. In Jesus' name. Amen.

Reflection

Day 3

CHOOSE TO OUTLIVE THE SEASON

Scriptural Text: *'For His anger endureth but a moment; in His favor is life: weeping may endure for a night, but joy cometh in the morning.'*

Psalm 30:5 (KJV)

Inspiring Commentary

Do you believe that life is full of ups and downs? That there are highs and lows. Moments of overwhelming joy and others of great sorrow? Why is this so? Because life is composed of diverse seasons. Daily existence isn't monotonous but full of surprises. So at one point, the surprises encountered can be pleasant; other times, they are unpleasant.

The good thing is that seasons are temporary. Every season runs its course and gives room for another. Therefore, there's a consolation even in seasons of sorrow and loss. What's the consolation? That the pain of loss and grief will pass. Just as seasons aren't designed to last forever, your pain isn't to last beyond its season.

As a result, no matter how hopeless your situation seems at the moment, you can find solace in knowing that it's only a season. Rather than be overwhelmed by the difficulties accompanying the season of grief, decide to outlive it. God has designed seasons to come and go but has given humans the ability to outlive seasons.

Some people who didn't know this truth allowed themselves to be conquered by the pressures around them. Little did they know that God created them with the ability to start again. When a chapter of life is complete, with God, you can begin a new chapter. It's true; there are seasons where you'll lose something or someone you cherished. However, there are many other seasons ahead of you where God fills your life with treasures in the form of people and achievements.

Sadly, few people make it through to their breakthrough and compensation seasons. I share some thoughts in my book, *The Other Side of Grief* from today's text, I expressed that "the night can't last forever, and the pain of losing a loved one can't last forever. You need to see this truth: your pain and sorrow will pass.

It doesn't matter to what extent you love a person; you can always move on in life without them. It's only God you can't live without. Therefore, you shouldn't think your world has been turned upside down and life has lost its meaning. Tell yourself that life still goes on. Realize that grief is part of the principle of time.

(Ecclesiastes 3:1-3 [KJV]) says, *"To every thing, there is a season, and a time to every purpose under the heaven: A time to be born, and a time to die; a time to plant, and a time to pluck up that which is planted; A time to kill, and a time to heal; a time to break down, and a time to build up;"* Because it is part of the principle of time, it'll come. Nevertheless, it will give way for another season or time to manifest. And without doubt, the season after mourning is the season of joy."[3]

Call to Action

- What are the thoughts and situations that have lasted for a long time in your life, and you desire that they come to an end in this season?

____

____

____

____

Prayer

Father, in the name of Jesus, I thank You for the validity of Your Word today. Now I know how temporal my grief is supposed to be. Now I understand that it always breaks into dawn no matter how dark the night is. And so I pray that You cause Your dawn into my life. Take away this night that seems to last forever and let my day dawn again. In Jesus' name. Amen.

Reflection

Day 4

COUNT YOUR BLESSINGS

Scriptural Text: *"Thank [God] in everything [no matter what the circumstances may be, be thankful and give thanks], for this is the will of God for you [who are] in Christ Jesus [the Revealer and Mediator of that will]."*

1 Thessalonians 5:18 (AMPC)

Inspiring Commentary

Have you noticed that human beings are more negative than positive? I bet you're familiar with the saying, "Hope for the best but prepare for the worst." What does this reveal? People are more likely to believe that something bad will happen than expect good things. But this mindset is contrary to God's plan for you. Such a pessimistic point of view makes it difficult to overcome setbacks or even grief.

God's Word teaches believers what to do in the worst situations. It's the same thing you're asked to do in the milk and honey seasons--count your blessings.

In our Scripture for today, God says, "Focus on the positives." He reveals that there's light within you even in thick darkness that can shine. No matter what's going on in your life, there's a blessing you can focus on to pull through. Yes, you might have lost someone special, but what about your memories with them? Are you seeing their presence in your life as a gift? Are you grateful to God that they crossed your path? Are you counting your blessings?

Counting your blessings is a way of life. It affects the way you perceive things. You can either focus on losing a loved one or appreciate God for the beauty they brought into your life. It's God's will that you're able to see the good in the bad and appreciate the blessing in what seems to be a curse. After all, the Bible says all things work together for your good. In my book, *The Other Side of Grief*, I shared some thoughts from Chris Pine who said, "'*The only thing you sometimes have control over is your perspective. You don't have control over your situation. But you have a choice about how you view it.*'[4]

It is difficult for a man to do beyond what he sees. Anything we experience is experienced from the lens of our perspectives. Your viewpoint must be transformed if you will overcome the problem of sadness and gloom that grief brings with it.

No one can give thanks for all things from a negative perspective. Indeed, only those who can see God at work behind the scenes can be optimistic. Those who count their blessings invite God not just to repeat the miracles of the past but to perform new miracles on their behalf."[5]

Call to Action

- What are the negative mindset you desire to replace with positive perspectives in your life?

____

____

____

____

Prayer

Father, in the name of Jesus, I thank You for the blessing of Your Word to me today. I submit my mind to You at this hour, praying that you renew my mind completely. Help me to think positively. I pray that I will always focus on the bright side of life and be grateful for the many blessings you have bestowed on me by Your Spirit. In Jesus' name. Amen.

Reflection

Day 5

THE PROMISE OF COMFORT

Scriptural Text: *'Blessed are they that mourn: for they shall be comforted.'*

Matthew 5:4 (KJV)

Inspiring Commentary

Do you remember the story of Job? He was an exceptional man who walked with God wholeheartedly. But when tragedy struck, Job did something any other person would do. He cursed the day he was born. It's so easy to see oneself as cursed when bad things happen. Losing a loved one casts a dark cloud over one's life, blocking out the rays of hope.

Believing you're cursed and that your loss is only the beginning of your sorrows hinders good from coming into your life. God doesn't want you to put such an awful label on yourself. Labels tie to one spot or occurrence, but you're more than that. You're not a product of what you've gone through but God's grace. Therefore, you can never be defined by your circumstances.

Job learned this lesson later when God gave him double everything he lost. Did he look like what he had been through? Of course not. This is why you must not see yourself as cursed and forsaken.

God still has a plan for you. Even in your season of mourning, He calls you blessed. Why are you blessed even in your pain and grief? Because of what God will do to compensate you. (Isaiah 61:7 [NIRV]) says, "*Instead of being put to shame you will receive a double share of wealth. Instead of being dishonored you will be glad to be in your land. You will receive a double share of riches there. And you'll be filled with joy that will last forever.*"

In my book, *The Other Side of Grief*, I shared these thoughts from today's text, "we understand that all Christians who mourn will be comforted by God; that's why they are blessed. Their comfort will be so great that although they were once to be pitied because of their sorrow, their joy will abound.

You must not see yourself as cursed or unlucky. Sadly, you lost someone so dear to you, but God can drown out the pain of your loss. He is ready to comfort you with His love and presence. God can fill your life with so much meaning and joy that your mourning will become a source of blessing. Consequently, see yourself as blessed because God has promised to comfort you.

Choose to see God's hand at work even in the darkest moments. This doesn't mean that you shouldn't cry your heart out and mourn your loved one. It just means it's not the end of the road for you. Loss is a part of life, even though no one desires to experience it. But since it has occurred, you can expect to receive a blessing from the Lord that will comfort you and take away the searing pain of grief."[6]

Seeing your situation through the lens of God's Word is the most effective way to overcome life's labels. So you can say to yourself, I'm blessed, not cursed. I'm not forsaken but comforted. As you speak these words in faith and trust God wilth all your heart to perform His Word, you will begin to see His blessings flow into every area of your life.

Call to Action

- What aspect of your life do you desire the comfort of the Holy Spirit?

____

____

- What truth have you discovered from Scriptures that have brought comfort to your soul?

Prayer

Father, in the name of Jesus, I thank You for the comfort that came to me from Your Word today. I thank You because I am not alone even in this gloomy season of my life. I pray that You comfort me on every side as You have promised. I pray that You give me peace like a river and double joy for the sorrow I have experienced. In Jesus' name. Amen.

Reflection

Day 6

DISCOVERING LIGHT IN DARKNESS

Scriptural Text: *For God, who commanded the light to shine out of darkness, hath shined in our hearts, to give the light of the knowledge of the glory of God in the face of Jesus Christ.*

2 Corinthians 4:6 (KJV)

Inspiring Commentary

It is impossible to know and appreciate the power of light without darkness. Why? Because the presence of darkness creates the need for light. And without darkness, the light won't be important. There'll be moments of darkness in your life. They don't come to destroy you but to cause the emergence of light. But the question is, how does the light show up out of darkness?

Wherever darkness is found, there's a potential for light. God doesn't need to create light; rather, He commands it to shine out of the darkness. The bad occurrences in your life represent darkness, while the good ones represent light. So when darkness comes, you have light to hold on to.

Sometimes, you need to discover the potential of light hidden under the cover of darkness. Through gratitude, you can leverage the good things in your life to overcome the power of negative occurrences, like the loss of someone dear.

Psychology can't solve the problem of grief. Only light can help you overcome it. The good news is that God has hidden light in the same occurrence that caused you pain. But how do you discover light in the darkness? Gratitude!

In my book, *The Other Side of Grief,* I shed some insights from Melody Beattie quote which says, "Gratitude makes sense of our past, brings peace for today, and creates a vision for tomorrow.' The memories of your loved ones are blessings you should be grateful for. Truth is, no one lives forever. What's important is the way you live and your impact on others.

Gratitude is first to God for giving you that loved one as a gift. (Job 1:21) says, '*And [Job] said, Naked came I out of my mother's womb, and naked shall I return thither: the LORD gave, and the LORD hath taken away; blessed be the name of the LORD.*' These were Job's words when he learned that his children were dead. He wasn't accusing God of being responsible for his loss; rather, he acknowledged God's sovereignty even in the situation. Instead of questioning God, he thanked God, who gave him children in the first place. How often do we mourn the loss of those we love and forget to appreciate their existence in our lives.

After lifting up your gratitude to God, you should have gratitude towards the person you've lost for the beauty and value they added to your life. Why gratitude when your heart is broken? Well, losing a loved one is devastating. But that's not the greatest tragedy. The greatest tragedy is never to have known love. People lose loved ones and begin to despise the lovely memories they had. This shouldn't be so. Memories are the souvenirs of relationships that are no more. Friend, from now start to draw sighs of fulfillment, broad smiles, and uncontrollable laughter."[7]

Call to Action

- I know you are experiencing heaviness now. I want you to think of what you are most grateful for regarding your past.

____

____

____

____

Prayer

Father, in the name of Jesus, I chose to express my gratitude to You for this day for Your mercy and goodness. I know that You are All-knowing while my sight is limited. I pray that You help me to remain grateful always. I ask that You cause Your light to shine out of the darkness in my life. I am grateful for the peace that comes from You. In Jesus' name. Amen.

Reflection

Day 7

DON'T TRASH YOUR FAITH

Scriptural Text: *But Jesus looked at them and said to them, "With men this is impossible, but with God all things are possible."*

Mathew 19:26 (NKJV)

Inspiring Commentary

The loss of a person can indeed feel like the loss of the future. You might wonder, "Where can I go from here?" "What will I do without my spouse?" "Who do I smile and share my deepest thought with?" "Will I ever recover from this loss?"

There's only one thing that can guarantee your answer to these questions. Your faith in God. A man once said to Jesus, *"If you have the ability, please heal my son."* He was putting all the responsibility on Jesus. But Jesus placed the responsibility back in his hands and said, *"If you can believe, all things are possible to him who believes."* (Mark 9:23)

In overcoming the storm of grief, you have the responsibility of faith in God. Fortunately, the Bible shows us God's track record and many reasons to trust Him even in hopeless situations. So, you have a choice to keep complaining or trust God for a way out. (Exodus 15:22-25 [NRIV]) says, *"Then Moses led Israel away from the Red Sea. They went into the Desert of Shur. For three days they traveled in the desert. They didn't find any water there. When they came to Marah, they couldn't drink its water. It was bitter. That's why the place is named Marah. The people told Moses they weren't happy with him. They said, "What are we supposed to drink?" Then Moses cried out to the* Lord. *The* Lord *showed him a stick. Moses threw it into the water. The water became fit to drink. There the Lord gave a ruling and instruction for the people. And there he tested them."*

Can you imagine the faith level of people who saw the ten plagues and countless miracles God performed for their sake? Concerning the Israelites, (Psalm 78:42 [AMP]) says, *"They did not remember [the miracles worked by] His [powerful] hand, Nor the day when He redeemed them from the enemy."* So, no matter the pain of the present, never forget the victories God won for you. Why? Because they guarantee future victories.

In my book, *The Other Side of Grief*, I shared, "You don't have to be like the Israelites, who always complained when they encountered difficulty even though they had seen mighty miracles. Understand that God can compensate you for the friend, parent, spouse, or child you lost. It's not enough to have hope of being reunited. You must believe that God still wants you to live a fulfilled life.

Yes, you might not want to replace these people, and God doesn't want that. But don't you realize that He brought these people into your life? Therefore, He's willing to bring more relationships and meaningful partnerships your way. This is so true. You might think, but it won't be the same. Well, God never does the same thing in the same way. He does better."[8]

Call to Action

- What effort are you putting into building your faith?

____

____

____

____

Prayer

Father, in the name of Jesus, I thank You for the truth of Your Word today. Thank You for keeping me on my feet despite the pressure around me. I pray that You help me to remain strong in my faith. I pray for the grace to take responsibility for my faith to grow in You. I pray that in the name of Jesus, my faith shall not fail. In Jesus' name. Amen.

Reflection

Day 8

LEVERAGING HOPE TO OVERCOME GRIEF

Scriptural Text: *For to him that is joined to all the living, there is hope: for a living dog is better than a dead lion.*

Ecclesiastes 9:4 (KJV)

Inspiring Commentary

Have you ever wondered why we can have dreams? We've never been to the future, yet we are sure it exists. Also, we seem sure that it'll be better than the present. So what powers dreams or positive expectations concerning the future? The answer is hope. Hope is God's investment in your heart that assures you of the future. Although you haven't seen it yet, you believe in its reality and begin to journey towards it.

Hope is one of life's currencies. It's impossible to live successfully without leveraging hope. Think about it. You use the force called hope every time you go to bed. You don't go to bed scared that you'll die. Even though you know your will has nothing to do with seeing the next day, you hope to wake up in the morning.

Now, beyond being one of the currencies of this life, hope is a product of the Christian faith. (Ephesians 2:12 [NLT]) says, *"In those days you were living apart from Christ. You were excluded from citizenship among the people of Israel, and you did not know the covenant promises God had made to them. You lived in this world without God and without hope."* It's your status as a child of God that gives you hope towards God.

The kind of hope that transcends the limitations and uncertainties of natural life.

Indeed, the hope you get from God as a believer goes beyond life on earth and is a force for overcoming grief. (1 Corinthians 15:19 [AMP]) says, *"If we who are [abiding] in Christ have hoped only in this life [and this is all there is], then we are of all people most miserable and to be pitied."* Misery and pity are the lots of those who don't have hope of eternity. At the same time, everyone who has Christ is guaranteed eternity with Him. This hope extends to your loved ones who died in faith. Therefore, when a Christian loses a loved one, such loss shouldn't produce misery reflecting hopelessness.

I shared in my book, *The Other Side of Grief* that, "The Bible doesn't teach that Christians shouldn't grieve those they've lost; far from it. Believers are asked even to weep and mourn with others who weep and mourn (Romans 12:15). However, in your grief, you're asked to be mindful that you should be different from the unbelievers. Why? Because of hope.

The joy of the Lord is a spiritual substance that can exist through hope even amid great sorrow. The hope that the temporary separation from your loved ones brings you joy. Those in the world grieve bitterly and harm themselves because they have nothing to look forward to in the days ahead. However, you know that you will be reunited with your loved ones as long as you're in Christ. Therefore, your grief for your temporary loss, but you're not overcome with grief."[9]

Thich Nhat Hanh once said, "*hope is important because it can make the present moment less difficult to bear. If we believe that tomorrow will be better, we can bear a hardship today.*"[10]

Call to Action

- What hope have you discovered from God's Word that is sufficient to retain joy in your heart?

____

____

____

____

Prayer

Father, in the name of Jesus, I thank You for the sure hope I have in You. I thank You because You remain a standing pillar around my life even when everything seems to fall apart. I pray that You help me walk in the reality of my hope in You. Help me to know that it doesn't all end here, but there is joy on the other side with You. I pray that by the Holy Spirit, You will keep the fire of hope alive in me. In Jesus' name. Amen.

Reflection

____

____

____

____

____

____

____

____

Day 9

FIGHT FROM WITHIN

Scriptural Text: *Fight a good fight for the faith and claim eternal life. God offered it to you when you clearly told about your faith while so many people listened.*

1 Timothy 6:12 (CEV)

Inspiring Commentary

Most of the battles we fight on the outward find their roots deep within us. And instead of choosing the right tools to fight off these battles, we turn to weak outward efforts. After trying so hard in the flesh for months; and years, even for others, we fall back into the hands of God where we should have taken our queues from in the first place. It's easy to locate and deal with any external problems and threats in our lives, but less or no attention is given to them when it comes to internal battles.

This is because we could veil internal wounds with outward smiles. People may be dying on the inside and yet wear a good smile. Whereas there are battles one could fight alone and secretly, others are better fought within the loving fellowship of believers. However, I strongly believe that the cure for inwards wounds is the urgent application of God's love. One of those internal wounds people carry through their lives is grief. Grief is a soul sickness that demands internal fight and victory.

In my book, *The Other Side of Grief*, I wrote that "Just as we have sicknesses for the body, we have for the soul and spirit too, and given that a man's life flows from the inside out, they are more challenging to identify, surmount and overcome. While there are sicknesses of the soul that are mild and minor, there are some that are malignant and pandemic. These malignant and pandemic "soul-sicknesses" reach out to the very core of one's being, and like a dementor, it sucks out life from that individual while such a person is still alive.

Of all the destructive "soul pandemics," grief is one of the most destructive. The destruction that grief brings does not come from it alone but with the things it brings. Grief is like a light stealer; it comes with gloom, pain, regret, anguish, blame, and instability. When grief hits an individual, it first kills all that person's spiritual and mental 'antibodies,' it destroys your mental immune system and leaves you vulnerable to every other emotional imbalance and trauma."[11] So, take hold of the hammer of the Word, and fight from within. Build capacity in the spirit and strengthen yourself from the inside out with praise.

Call to Action

- What are the wounds you have inside that you need God to help you heal up and fight for you?

____

____

____

____

Prayers

Father, in the name of Jesus, I thank You for the truth of Your Word today. Thank You for showing me that I am not a loser but a winner. I thank You for the victory I have in You. I pray for the grace to fight every grief and sadness in my heart. I receive the boldness and the capacity to stop the trend of grief around me. My spirit man is fired up into new life today. In Jesus' name. Amen.

Reflection

Day 10

WE ALL LOSE SOMETIMES

Scriptural Text: *Rejoice not against me, O mine enemy: when I fall, I shall arise; when I sit in darkness, the LORD shall be a light unto me.*

Micah 7:8 (KJV)

Inspiring Commentary

Have you ever lost something you crave you could get back? What about someone who were dear and close to your heart? I bet you have! We've all lost something or someone at one point or another. And many times, some loss hits deeply and leaves us broken and shattered, unable to move on. Just like me, have you ever wanted death to never happen? What if we never die? What if there's no evil in the world? And everyone we've ever loved stays with us forever.

Well, that kind of world is impossible where men are free-will agents. You do not need to be an unbeliever to be a victim of grief and pain that comes with loss. Christian grieve too! Grief is an archetypal experience of man, where you live notwithstanding. When left unattended, many believers die quietly, not facing the facts with the shield of faith. Yes, it's normal to grieve, but allowing loss and experience to hinder future hopes and present fulfillment is destructive.

Even though we all go through ugly experiences in life, how we see and get over them differs. This is where what makes one stronger could become why another loses every sense of humor. Not letting go of painful or beautiful memories of the past to usher in the future could be deadly cancer within.

In my book, *The Other Side of Grief*, I wrote that "Grief sits so deep into the core of a person's soul that it starts defining everything about such a person. It works this way; it looks like the normal thing to do when grieving. At least, after a loss, it is human to feel bad and remorseful, but that's not it; it's just the beginning.

You start feeling like a traitor for trying to forget memories that cause you pain and anguish. One moment, you want to forget the object of your grief and "move on," but then you tell yourself that those memories (the same ones that cause you pain) are all you have about that person, and you just won't let them go. The same you that needs a break is the one who feels like resuming your "suspended" life."[12] So, keep the fire of hope and joy alive and learn to move on to greater victory.

Call to Action

- What are the struggles you are experiencing regarding letting go of your challenges?

____

____

____

____

Prayer

Father, in the name of Jesus, I thank You for the reality of Your Word today. I pray that You help me not to remain in a sense of hopelessness with my loss. I know loss is part of life. I pray that You strengthen me to move forward despite the loss. I pray that You help me stay focused and dedicated to my purpose in life despite the loss I have experienced. In Jesus' name. Amen.

Reflection

Day 11

REGAINING CONTROL OVER YOUR LIFE

Scriptural Text: *"For dominion belongs to the Lord, and He rules over the nations."*

Psalm 22:28 (KJV)

Inspiring Commentary

You get a sense of control from hard work and intensive planning. You can determine the kind of life you want, your career, the number of kids you'll have, your friends, and even where you'll live. You can decide what your days look like by having a routine. Also, your choices today affect your future so that you can control the future in a way. But in truth, all these things give you only a sense of control.

Many things in life are beyond your control. A million things can happen to affect the sanity of your world. One of them is the loss of a loved one which sometimes causes things to spiral out of control, and you begin to wonder if you were ever in control. You lose that sense of control you've always had when this happens.

In my book, *The Other Side of Grief*, I share that, "Human beings are creatures of dominion. God created us to have authority, so we naturally desire control. When we hold all the cards, we're more hopeful and happy. But the loss of control sets off an alarm in us that causes a state of pandemonium. One of the greatest causes of fear for someone who grieves is losing control.

Isn't it interesting how everyone thinks they're in control until they realize they aren't? Even people with great power and influence aren't safe from the greedy fingers of death. They die of terminal diseases and accidents and even get assassinated. Death gives us a rude wake-up call, calling our bluff. It says, 'Your sense of control is a sham.' Naturally, this causes a great deal of fear.

God desires that you live in boldness and not fear, believing that the worst could happen. He wants you to believe in the future, knowing that your kids will graduate college, your career will be successful, and the goals you've set will be reached. But it's hard to unlearn what grief has taught you about control. Indeed, no human being is in control of their life or the lives of their loved ones. Therefore, how can you live without fear and have faith in the future?"[13]

Realizing that you're not in control is a blessing, not a curse. It makes you turn to the only person who truly has control over life, God. Look at (Jeremiah 10:23 [ESV]): *"I know, O LORD, that man's way is not in himself, that it is not in man who walks to direct his steps."* The only way to regain control in your life is to lose it to God. The Scriptures reveal that man's sense of control isn't real. True control over life is with God; our role is to surrender to God and trust Him to run our lives.

Call to Action

- What are the areas you know you no longer have control over and you need to surrender to God?

____

____

____

____

Prayer

Father, in the name of Jesus, I thank You for Your Word to me today. I understand that I am created to have dominion. I pray that You will help me regain mastery over my thoughts and life. Holy Spirit, I ask that You take control over every aspect of my life that I have handled alone till now. I pray that You take away every fear from my heart. In Jesus' name. Amen.

Reflection

Day 12

OVERCOMING THE FEELING OF LONELINESS

Scriptural Text: *"When you pass through the waters, I will be with you. When you cross rivers, you will not drown. When you walk through fire, you will not be burned, nor will the flames hurt you."*

Isaiah 43:2 (NCV)

Inspiring Commentary

I shared in my book, *The Other Side of Grief*, "One of the most powerful and most dangerous emotions stirred up by grief is loneliness. This is because you once had someone with whom you faced every challenge. Whether a sibling, spouse, or parent, that person made you feel safe and supported. You knew you weren't alone. However, it leaves a gaping hole in your heart when death takes them away. For a while, you'll be in denial. You won't want to be comforted or even believe they are gone.

No matter how much that tear in your heart hurts, you won't want it to be healed at first. All you want is for your loved one to walk back into your life, telling you it was a bad dream. This attitude causes you to push away everyone that tries to help. Sometimes you might feel they want to erase your loved one's memory or replace them. Grief pushes us into isolation yet causes us to dread being alone forever. We wonder if we'll ever feel the connection we once have with that person or recover from our loss."[14]

The Bible teaches believers that they're not alone, even in the worst situation. God promises never to forsake you. He had to make this promise because you live in a world where those you counted on can turn their backs on you. Even those who are loyal can be snatched away by death. And those who admire you can forsake you when you're no longer successful or attractive.

God is the only Father and friend whose presence is constant. So even in the season of grief where you feel so alone, He's there. (Deuteronomy 31:8 [NIV]) says, *"The LORD Himself goes before you and will be with you; He will never leave you nor forsake you. Do not be afraid; do not be discouraged."* Are you wondering what your life would become without those you've lost? Do you feel like a part of you was ripped out, and you'll never be the same? God says He's with you. He's not going anywhere, and He's also not giving up on you.

Remember (Isaiah 43:2 [NET]) says, *"When you pass through the waters, I am with you; when you pass through the streams, they will not overwhelm you. When you walk through the fire, you will not be burned; the flames will not harm you."* The loneliness you feel doesn't tell the truth about your circumstances. God is with you and is willing to fill the vacuum you feel in your heart.

God brings people into your life to bless you or make you a blessing. But He doesn't want you to depend on them for wholeness. Wholeness comes from God and not from people. Once you begin to see that God was the source of everything you got from your loved ones and they were only channels, you'll turn to God to fill the void they left.

Call to Action

- Who are the people in your life that you depend on, and feel as tho you may not recover if you lose them?

____

____

____

____

- What have you discovered about the everlasting comfort of the Lord in your life?

____

____

____

____

Prayer

Father, in the name of Jesus, I thank You for the assurance You have sent me from Your Word today. I thank You for the comfort of Your presence with me always. I pray that You will help me move on and embrace Your presence with me. I know I cannot have the company of my loved one again. But today, I submit to Your sure company. Help me to understand that You are with me always. In Jesus' name. Amen.

Reflection

____

____

____

____

____

____

____

____

Day 13

RECEIVING HELP FROM GOD'S WORD

Scriptural Text: *His Word is quick and powerful, sharper than any two-edged sword, piercing to the dividing asunder of the soul and spirits and of the joints and marrows, and it discerns the thoughts and intents of the heart. This is to show you how potent the Word of God is.*

Hebrews 4:12 (ESV)

Inspiring Commentary

As a human being, you'll always come to a point where you need someone's help. This is because humans are designed to depend on each other. However, some problems are beyond the scope of human help. In such circumstances, you need God's help. And to receive and enjoy God's help, you need to know how He provides it.

(2 Peter 1:3 [KJV]) says, "*...His divine power has given us all things that pertain to life and godliness, through the knowledge of Him who called us by glory and virtue.*" This Scripture reveals that everything you'll ever need for natural or spiritual life is hidden in God's Word for you. God sends you help via His Word, just as you visit the bank to get a loan. You can't get the loan without going to the bank. So you need to know God's Word concerning your situation. God's Word is the treasure house of His resources.

Thus, those who haven't devoted their lives to God's Word will never access the treasures stored up for them. Some people go through life blaming God for not providing for them or caring enough to help them? Whereas, He has provided for all things.

Do you know how He could provide for all things? Because He knows everything you need, right down to the most minute detail. (Hebrews 4:15 [AMP]) says, *"For we do not have a High Priest who is unable to sympathize and understand our weaknesses and temptations, but One who has been tempted [knowing exactly how it feels to be human] in every respect as we are..."*

In my book, *The Other Side of Grief*, I shared some comforting thoughts that, "God is not oblivious of all the feelings that go through your mind. He is concerned with everything that happens to you and how you respond to them. This is why no matter what you're going through, God has something to say concerning it. His words are not just letters stringed together; they are power and life. And that is why He gives His Word to every situation to help you overcome.

The Word of God is the ultimate panacea given by God over any situation. No matter the circumstance, God is saying something. The quickness and power of His Word are demonstrated in that His Word provides whatever you need.[15] Stay with the Word until it revives your spirit. Don't stop there once your spirit is revived. Stay hungry and thirsty for His Word!

Call to Action

- Develop a plan to study God's Word consistently and at all times.

____

____

____

____

Prayer

Father, in the name of Jesus, I thank You for life in Your Word always. Thank You for the Spirit content of Your Word that can revive my spirit. I pray for the grace to see the truth in Your Word always. I pray that through Your Spirit, let the quickening power of Your Word stir me up from sadness into joy unlimited. In Jesus' name. Amen.

Reflection

Day 14

OVERCOMING UNCERTAINTY ABOUT THE FUTURE

Scriptural Text: *"Those who trust in the LORD are like Mount Zion, which cannot be shaken but endures forever."*

Psalm 125:1 (KJV)

Inspiring Commentary

I shared in my book, *The Other Side of Grief* that, "Losing a loved one ushers in uncertainty because your life seemed to have order and purpose, but death disrupted everything. When a loved one dies, they don't go alone. The dreams, plans, goals, and hopes you shared also die. And even if they don't die completely, pursuing them without the person who was such an integral part of it causes anxiety.

Sometimes, you might even wonder if those plans will ever be achieved. Once a tragedy occurs and place another obstacle on your part? You might even feel like plans are useless because no one can truly determine the future. After all, you're a witness to that fact.

There's confidence and motivation that comes with certainty. You're encouraged and inspired to make sacrifices, take risks, and attempt incredible feats. But when fear comes in through the door of loss and grief, life becomes a shaky foundation you don't want to risk building anything on."[16]

Are you uncertain about the future? Do you expect life to throw you another curveball? Have you decided that there's no point in chasing dreams and falling in love because you can lose everything? The truth is, you can never find certainty in this world. Why? Because the structure of this reality is delicate. It was designed to be temporary, subject to change--easily altered by circumstances.

(2 Corinthians 4:18 [AMP]) says, *"So we look not at the things which are seen, but at the things which are unseen; for the things which are visible are temporal [just brief and fleeting], but the things which are invisible are everlasting and imperishable."* This visible world and the life that revolves around it is temporal. You can't find certainty here.

But there's good news! You can find certainty in God. The Bible calls God our rock. (Isaiah 44:8 [NASB]) says, *"Do not tremble and do not be afraid; Have I not long since announced it to you and declared it? And you are My witnesses. Is there any God besides Me, or is there any other Rock? I know of none."*

Why is God referred to as a rock? Because He's stable, consistent, trustworthy, and a firm foundation for our lives. With Him, the future isn't uncertain because He knows it. God is your protection from the uncertainty of life

Take your eyes off the loss and pain, and focus on God. You can trust Him with the future. Our text today reveals that those who trust God will experience divine stability in their life. They will be certain of their future in an uncertain world. The secret is trust.

After the loss you've experienced, are you willing to trust God with your life, career, and loved ones? Although it is often said, "Don't put all your eggs in one basket," with God, that's the only way. You have to trust Him with all your heart. (Proverbs 3:5) Give all your uncertainty to God and allow Him to guide you into a glorious future.

Call to Action

- What can you see about your tomorrow from God's words that negate what you are going through?

Prayer

Father, in the name of Jesus, I thank You for the stability of Your Word and the authenticity of Your promises. I pray that You keep me stable with Your Word. I know my future is secured in Your hand. Therefore, I pray for the grace to see the light at the end of the tunnel of grief I'm in. I pray that You will see me through into my colorful future. In Jesus' name. Amen.

Reflection

Day 15

GOD HAS SOMETHING TO SAY

Scriptural Text: *I will hear what God the LORD will speak: for He will speak peace unto His people, and to His saints...*

Psalm 85:8 (KJV)

Inspiring Commentary

God still has something to say when grief makes you gloomy, worried and hurt. This might not make sense, but God always has something to say, and cases of grief are not an exception. The masterpiece of God is aware of everything a man goes through; amazingly, grief is part of the curriculum. Given that we as humans experience certain losses and pain at one point or the other. However, God's not unaware of this; we do not have a High priest that does not sympathize with our weaknesses and frailties. Although He is God, He came in the form of a human as Jesus to experience what it's like to live on the earth so that He can make available the office of strength for trying times like this.

In my book, *The Other Side of Grief*, I share that, "No matter what you're going through, God has something to say concerning it. His words are not just letters stringed together. They are power and life. And that is why He gives His Word towards every situation to help you overcome."[17] News flash, God, is not only aware of this grief, but He's also infusing strength, He's quickening your mortal bodies, and He's subtly speaking to you to heal you and help you overcome this phase through the power in His Word.

How does He speak in this season? He speaks through His Word to your inner man to equip you with every strength needed to overcome the phase because we have an understanding that His words are not just letters strung together, but they are Spirit and they are life. These words can permeate through the ditch of grief and birth joy because there is an understanding of greater peace and greater glory.

While the devil's major assignment is to allow grief and pain to sink into you so much that you don't have access to the reality of joy in God, and the noise, pressure cloud you, and both solicited and unsolicited advice from society. Instead, you must hold on to the office of strength in God and ask Him, God, what are you saying?"[18] Because right now, my ears are open, and I desire to hear You above every other opinion of men. God is not talkative, but He understands the gross impact of His Word on your body, soul, and spirit this season, and He yearns for you, amazingly, much more than you do for Him.

Call to Action

- What has God spoken to you since you found yourself in the well of grief?

____

____

____

____

- If not, take a pen and paper and maintain an open heart whenever you study the Word and pray. You can use this space below to get started.

____

____

____

____

Prayers

Father, thank You for always speaking to me as You have done today. Thank You for not leaving me to my condition and not letting go of me. I pray that You open my heart to receive Your Word and open my ear to hear You. I pray that You help me to hear Your instruction regarding the way out of my challenges and grief. In Jesus' name. Amen.

Reflection

Day 16

GRIEF IS SUBTLE

Scriptural Text: *"Blessed be God, even the Father of our Lord Jesus Christ, the Father of mercies, and the God of all comfort; Who comforteth us in all our tribulation, that we may be able to comfort them which are in any trouble, by the comfort wherewith we ourselves are comforted of God."*

2 Corinthians 1:3-4 (KJV)

Inspiring Commentary

Grief possesses no identity; rather, it lurks around negative emotions and tries to find expression via this platform. For instance, when a person is sick, we are all aware that this person is going through a physiological disorder in his body. Sometimes, the result of this sickness to the loved ones around him is grief, they are sapped of their strength, and they are filled with so much worry that they show care and concern out of grief. So, grief cannot possess someone without inflicting an affliction, loss, or pain. It doesn't have the luxury of being identified as a component.

I explained in my book, *The Other Side of Grief* that, "Grief does not have an identity; it comes hidden under other things like loss, pain, guilt, and disappointment. It does not come straight at you as other strong emotions do; it comes tender, almost naturally; you would almost think it's normal till it starts seeping through your mind and removing all the light of positivity it is left. By the time you accept that you're grieving, you're already used to what it brings."[19]

Amazingly, you permit this ploy and tactics of the devil to always get away into you, encapsulating your spirit, soul, and body with grief through different means. Just like grief comes subtly, overcoming it must also come gradually. In minor cases where issues that could birth grief arise, you must advertently rebuke it and find succor in the words of the Lord. The Bible says, *"Blessed be the God and Father of our Lord Jesus Christ, the Father of mercies and God of all comfort, who comforts us in all our affliction, so that we may be able to comfort those who are in any affliction, with the comfort with which we ourselves are comforted by God."* (2 Corinthians 1:3-4) You must not allow the subtle and non-identified power of grief to permeate you when the Comforter is by your side. The Comforter is raising you as a comforter to other persons. The devil, aware of these plans, wants to ruin this process and place both you and the lives in your care into continuous and consistent grief.

Call to Action

- In what way(s) have you been deceived through the subtlety of grief to remain in sorrow and mourning.

____

____

____

____

Prayer

Father, in the name of Jesus, I thank You for exposing the subtleness of grief to me today. I pray that You open my eyes to the deceptive feeling that holds me back from experiencing the fullness of Your joy and peace. I will no longer give room to the devil's tactics to hold me back from my purpose by using the bait of grief. In Jesus' name. Amen.

Reflection

Day 17

ENGAGE THE SPIRIT OF GOD

Scriptural Text: *"Now the Lord is the Spirit; and where the Spirit of the Lord is, there is liberty."*

2 Corinthians 3:17 (KJV)

Inspiring Commentary

God's words say in (2 Timothy 1:7 [KJV]), *"For God hath not given us the spirit of fear, but of power, love, and a sound mind."* When the Word, Spirit of God, is mentioned, what comes to mind is not fear, not grief or bondage. Rather the Scripture says in (2 Corinthians 3:17 [KJV]), *"Now the Lord is the Spirit; and where the Spirit of the Lord is, there is liberty."* Liberty does not include grief; to be grievous is to be a slave to pain and sadness. Paul, a servant of God who has suffered for the gospel in different ways, was able to affirmatively state, *"For I reckon that the sufferings of this present time are not worthy to be compared with the glory which shall be revealed in us." (*Romans 8:18) Paul was able to make this statement because he has engaged with the Word of God; therefore, grief couldn't consume him irrespective of what he goes through. He understands that these sufferings are temporary; there is a joy and glory ahead that is eternal.

In my book, *The Other Side of Grief*, I asked, "Do you seek to experience joy as a river? Simply engage the Spirit of God. Let Him help you through the storms and turmoils of life. The Spirit of God is released by God to help believers through life, to help us as we seek to know God more and become like Him. His Spirit is there to help you through it all!" The Spirit of God cannot be caught unawares; first, it is a Spirit, and second, it is of God. So, it possesses the whole package needed to overcome grief; this Spirit understands whichever ploy or method the devil wants to use. Because of your consistent engagement with the Spirit, He resides in you; He informs you ahead and gives you a higher strategy to override the power of grief.

The Spirit of God is potent for every life situation, including overcoming grief, but until you engage it, you might not see this reality. The Spirit of God is a parcel that contains every package and victuals needed to overcome grief. To not engage this Spirit is to short-change yourself and express liberty to the devil. So, do well to communicate with the Holy Spirit in prayers and pour your heart to Him whenever you feel the heaviness."[20]

Call to Action

- Develop a plan to always engage the Holy Spirit and pray in tongues.

- Are you yet to be baptized in the Holy Spirit? Close your door and open your heart for the infilling of the Spirit. Start by calling out the names of God!

Prayer

Father, in the name of Jesus, I thank You for the understanding I have received from Your Word today; I pray that You will help me walk in Your Spirit's liberty. I am no longer a slave to fear my loss or the past. I am no longer a slave to grief anymore, but I begin to walk in the liberty of Jesus. Holy Spirit, take your place in my heart afresh and see me through every challenge I face right now. In Jesus' name. Amen.

Reflection

Day 18

NO DOCTOR CAN MEND A BROKEN HEART

Scriptural Text: *"A cheerful heart is good medicine, but a broken spirit saps a person's strength."*

Proverbs 17:22 (NLT)

Inspiring Commentary

The heart is an internal organ and a vital part of the human body. It performs a significant role necessary for the successful running of the body. However, this same heart that looks and posits itself as a premium part of the body sometimes feels weak. To explain the state of one's heart when feeling weak, discouraged, tired, or worn out, we say your heart is broken. No doctor here on earth can fix or mend a broken heart. When the heart is broken, it begins to hurt the external part of the physical body. More reason, the Scripture records that *"A cheerful heart is good medicine, but a broken spirit saps a person's strength."* (Proverbs 17:22)

I shared in my book, *The Other Side of Grief* that, "Anyone who grieves has a broken heart. Expert physicians can mend broken bodies, but a broken heart can't be mended. Why? Aren't their physicians who are heart specialists? Yes, of course. However, a broken heart isn't a physical problem that can be cured by fixing the organ called the heart." Medical doctors don't have the luxury of mending a broken heart; only God can fix that. When a heart is broken, courtesy of grief, pain, or loss, it cannot contain joy, happiness, or any other positive emotion because of its broken state. If joy or anything of such is deposited inside the heart, it leaks off within a few minutes because the heart is leaking. And the doctors of this earth can't fix it.

While Jesus Christ was leaving the earth, He promised to send the Comforter to the disciples, emphasizing that He would not leave them as orphans. The role of a comforter is to comfort; Christ was aware of the different phases and areas in which we as humans will need the role of the Comforter, more reason He stated it explicitly. It is above men's jurisdiction to mend a broken heart; God has the power to heal sicknesses of our body and mend the broken heart."[21] Your heart is safe in God's hand, and He will mend it appropriately.

Call to Action

- What areas of your life are broken, and you need the mending hand of God? It's time to pray about it.

____

____

____

____

Prayer

Father, in the name of Jesus, I thank You for the medicinal dose of Your Word today. I surrender myself to Your theatre of healing. I know I can't do it on my own. I know I can't mend my broken heart. I pray that You heal me, oh God. I pray that Your Spirit will work through me from the inside out and let me experience Your healing hand in my life. In Jesus' name. Amen.

Reflection

Day 19

BEAUTY FOR ASHES

Scriptural Text: *"I have told you all this so that you may have peace in me. Here on earth you will have many trials and sorrows. But take heart, because I have overcome the world."*

John 16:33 (NLT)

Inspiring Commentary

A phrase usually attributed to God's sovereign power; it says, "you give beauty for ashes." Ashes mean dust, remain from fire, and there is nothing beautiful about ashes, but the Scripture brings explicitly to our notice how God can bring beauty out of ashes. It simply means regardless of the situation, God can cause a shift and turnaround. This informs us that God is aware, He is aware that on some days, you'd be so down and weak, but He's working something out for your good, thereby helping you to recuperate and overcome grief.

In my book, *The Other Side of Grief*, I shared from (Isaiah 61:3 [KJV]) which says, *"To appoint unto them that mourn in Zion, to give unto them beauty for ashes, the oil of joy for mourning, the garment of praise for the spirit of heaviness; that they might be called trees of righteousness, the planting of the LORD, that He might be glorified."* God is aware that even in Zion, at certain times, there are people that mourn because of one loss or the other, and there is heaviness upon the souls of these persons. However, much more than His awareness, He promises to give beauty to ashes, praise garments, and gladness oil. Here is your solace and comfort, that you serve a God that isn't caught unaware by the situations of life and has also prepared everything needed to thrive in life.

Before His departure, Jesus said to His disciples, *"I have told you all this so that you may have peace in Me. Here on earth you will have many trials and sorrows. But take heart, because I have overcome the world.* (John 16:33 [NLT]) Grief is part of the world, Christ said; He has overcome it. So, my disposition is to dwell and abide in Christ so that I can enjoy the luxuries He has made available for me in Himself. What is it that is causing you grief?"[22] No matter how big or deep the pain is, God is set to give you the beauty in the place of grief because what grief does is taint and dent your beauty? In the place of grief, the Holy Spirit will renew your heart, position you to see reasons to rejoice and begin to flourish once again.

Call to Action

- What dimension of beauty do you desire from the Spirit of God?

____

____

____

____

Prayer

Father, in the name of Jesus, I thank You for the assurance of Your Word today. I understand that Your beauty can replace my ashes and dirt. I lay down my struggles before You. I come before You as broken and messed up as I am. And I pray that You beautify me again. No one comes to You and remains the same. I pray that You transform me and restore my beauty in Christ. Let my life radiate Your glory again. In Jesus' name. Amen.

Reflection

Day 20

YOUR PERSPECTIVE DETERMINES YOUR ATTITUDE

Scriptural Text: *As he calculates the cost to himself, this is what he does: He tells you, "Eat and drink," but he doesn't really mean it.*

Proverbs 23:7 (GW)

Inspiring Commentary

You can't be blessed more than what you see because it is what you see, either in the Scriptures, in sermons, dreams, and revelations, that you can sit with and ask for the reality to be made expressive in your life. So, your perspective has a role in all spheres of your life, including overcoming grief. A wise man once said, "you look like what you look at," and the Scriptures buttressing it said, *"Looking to Jesus, the Founder and Perfecter of our faith, who for the joy that was set before him endured the cross, despising the shame, and is seated at the right hand of the throne of God."* (Hebrews 12:2 [ESV]) Who and what we look at shape our perspective, and this, in turn, builds our attitude towards life.

I deliver these points from my book, *The Other Side of Grief* that, "Your perspective determines your attitude, and your attitude determines the quality of your life. In every situation, you can have either a negative or positive perspective. You're right if you say you've reached the end of your road. And if you say there's still hope for you, you're also right. Your perspective shapes your reality." What you believe, confess and profess goes a long way in establishing who you are. If the Scripture says, “Blessed are those who mourn, for they shall be comforted,” my view of this should be receiving the comfort to get blessed—processing a full understanding that my perspective shapes my reality.”[23]

Amid all the pain, loss, and grief, Job, in the Scripture, maintained communion and engagement with God; this ensured the right positioning of his perspective, thereby shaping his attitude in all the happenings around him. Grief couldn’t grip or encompass him because his perspective was set and deduced from God’s Word. You must always choose to see God’s hand at work, even in grief. Remember, it’s a choice, and it’s a choice made daily at the feet of the cross, even when everything says otherwise. You’re confident in who you believe, and you choose to see Him, thereby establishing your total victory over grief.

Call to Action

- In what way have you left off your commitment to God’s Word? It’s time to retrace your step.

____

____

____

____

- Get a pen and paper to write out instructions from the Word at all times. You can start below.

____

____

____

____

Prayer

Father, in the name of Jesus, I thank You for the truth of Your Word regarding my perspective. I thank You for the renewing power in Your Word. I pray that You transform me by Your Word. I pray that Your Word becomes my only standard of thought and action from this day forth. I dedicate my attitude to the teachings of Your Word. In Jesus' name. Amen.

Reflection

Day 21

AN ATTITUDE OF GRATITUDE

Scriptural Text: *Giving thanks always for all things unto God and the Father in the name of our Lord Jesus Christ;*

Ephesians 5:20 (KJV)

Inspiring Commentary

Thanksgiving is one of the most challenging things to do when experiencing grief birthed from loss. You're so weak and vexed in your spirit that you can't find the urge or desire to thank the Lord. However, it's a plot of the devil, the greatest adversary, to stop you from accessing what God is set to bring out of the situation. Gratitude is an attitude that must be cultivated not only when everything seems good and flourishing but also on days when the light seems dim. This is because gratitude opens you up and helps you take cognizance of the light within your reach.

In my book, *The Other Side of Grief*, I wrote that, "Gratitude is first to God for giving you that loved one as a gift. (Job 1:21) says, *"And [Job] said, Naked came I out of my mother's womb, and naked shall I return thither: the LORD gave, and the LORD hath taken away; blessed be the name of the LORD."* These were Job's words when he learned that his children were dead. He wasn't accusing God of their deaths but acknowledging God's sovereignty in permitting it to happen. Instead of questioning God, he thanked God, who gave him children in the first place. How often we mourn the loss of those, we love and forget to appreciate their existence in our lives." Gratitude does not necessarily bring back the things or relationships you've lost, but it equips you with the victuals needed to transform from that phase to the next phase."[24]

Job was a man like you and me, who experienced loss at its peak, yet he acknowledged the sovereign power of God. Offering gratitude makes sense of our past, brings peace for today, and creates a vision for tomorrow, says Melody Beattle. The presence of gratitude permits you to have a deep insight and cherish the memories of relationships that are no more. However, with grief, you despise the memories and drift into your shell, in fear of relating with others, and gradually you're encapsulated in bitterness, seeing nothing to be grateful for. There's always something to be thankful for; approaching grief with gratitude opens you to this understanding.

Call to Action

- What did you learn from Job's response and attitude of gratitude even with all the things that happened to him?

____

____

____

____

Prayer

Father, in the name of Jesus, I thank You for the light from Your Word today. I am grateful for everything. Thank You for keeping me sane and alive since I lost my loved one. I know You are Sovereign, and You understand even the very things that I cannot see or know. I am grateful because I know that everything works together for my good. Thank You, Father. In Jesus' name. Amen.

Reflection

Day 22

DON'T LOSE YOUR JOY TO THE STORM

Scriptural Text: *Even if the fig tree does not bloom and the vines have no grapes, even if the olive tree fails to produce and the fields yield no food, even if the sheep pen is empty and the stalls have no cattle— even then, I will be happy with Yahweh. I will truly find joy in God, who saves me.*

Habakkuk 3:17-18 (GW)

Inspiring Commentary

Grief is a raging storm that seeks to destroy everything in its path. Fortunately, grief can only access things in the physical. So, it can cause loss and pain. However, it cannot access spiritual substances like joy because it's located in your spirit. (Isaiah 12:3 [ESV]) says, *"With joy, you will draw water from the wells of salvation."*

Yet, the effects of grief in your life can make you shift your focus from that joy to the pain in the circumstance. You must fight to keep your joy no matter the situation. Why? Because joy is the currency for salvation. It gives you access to the manifold deliverances of God. The Scripture above didn't say you'll have access to a well, but wells.

In my book, *The Other Side of Grief*, I shared that, "Grief does not have an identity; it comes hidden under other things like loss, pain, guilt, and disappointment. It does not come straight at you as other strong emotions do; it comes tender, almost naturally; you would almost think it's normal until it starts seeping through your mind and removing all the light of positivity left. By the time you accept that you're grieving, you're already used to what it brings.

It is safest to understand that the first thing grief seeks to remove from an individual is joy, not happiness, as it were. What is the difference between joy and happiness? Happiness is an individual's response to pleasant situations, while joy is the indwelling faculty of serenity and tranquility.

When you lose someone and something, it's normal for you to be sad or lose your happiness for some time; what is wrong is that you allow your joy to wither. What is improper is that you allow grief to access your joy, bringing you despair and depression. What can one do when grief threatens to exhume all the joy within an individual?"[25]

The Bible gives them a seer in (Psalm 26:11) quoted above, '*...in the presence of God, there is fullness of joy.'* This implies that the only place in the world where joy flows without end is in God's presence. It is only in the presence of His being that one can radiate with joy and happiness without end."

In order for you to not to lose your joy to the storms of grief, you must learn to get into God's presence and stay there. Through constant fellowship with God and consciousness of His presence in your heart, you can preserve your joy in any situation.

Call to Action

- Describe how you have overcome sadness into a frequency of joy.

___

___

___

___

Prayer

Father, in the name of Jesus, I thank You for Your abiding presence with me always. I pray that You fill my heart with joy unspeakable, full of glory. I pray that I will no longer be weary or sad. I ask that through the inspiration of the Holy Spirit, You will feel my heart with joy and gladness. No more sadness around me in Jesus' name. Amen.

Reflection

Day 23

FEAR IS A PRISON WARDEN

Scriptural Text: *"God is a safe place to hide, ready to help when we need him. We stand fearless at the cliff-edge of doom, courageous in sea storm and earthquake; Before the rush and roar of oceans, the tremors that shift mountains. Jacob-wrestling God fights for us, God-of-Angel-Armies protects us."*

Psalm 46:1-3 (MSG)

Inspiring Commentary

You know how the approaching steps of a prison warden grip the prisoner; that's the role of fear. There won't be a need for a prison warden if one isn't in prison already. So, when the devil is certain that he has placed you in prison, he introduces the prison warden: fear; it drains you of hope and strips you of faith. The same Elijah who the Lord has used in conquering the prophets of Baal on Mount Carmel heard a threat from Jezebel and fled (1 Kings 19). This explicitly shows the detrimental effect of fear on the human mind, regardless of the previous achievement or sense of courage and boldness. Fear does not have two duties or roles in a man other than to rid you of your faith regardless of how long you've built such faith.

In my book, *The Other Side of Grief,* I explain that, "In the context of loss and grief, fear is a prison warden that wants to keep you in the chains of depression, pain, and gloom. It desires to drain you of hope and strip you of faith."[26] Fear is a spirit that is so harmful and destructive, so much so that the Scripture replaced it with three powerful virtues to subdue its potency. The Scripture says, *"For God hath not given us the spirit of fear, but of power, and of love, and of a sound mind."* (2 Timothy 1:7 [KJV]) The Scripture understands how fear can make one delusional and sensitive to unnecessary issues.

To permit the prison warden of fear to access you is to be stripped of your faith and gradually drift into paranoia. Fear is destructive. However, we have a much more word of truth; you must face the prison warden, fear, with all the faith you can gather within you. And even if the faith is as small as a mustard seed, it will still dislodge and dispel fear. Fear doesn't want you to see the light placed right at the end of the tunnel.

Call to Action

- List out your fears and the impact of fear on your life.

____

____

____

____

- What steps will you take to overcome the fears and break free?

____

____

____

____

Prayer

Father, in the name of Jesus, I understand that I have allowed fear to chain me and keep me depressed. Fear has made me anxious, and I can't see the joy ahead. I pray today that You take away fear from my heart and let Your boldness fill my heart. I am no longer a slave to my fears, but I am filled with the Spirit of God. In Jesus' name. Amen.

Reflection

Day 24

THE SECRET PLACE

Scriptural Text: *So whenever we are in need, we should come bravely before the throne of our merciful God. There we will be treated with undeserved kindness, and we will find help.*

Hebrews 4:16 (CEV)

Inspiring Commentary

The secret place sounds like a place where you go to fellowship and draw strength before appearing in public. It sounds that way, but that is also what it is. A secret place is a place of renewal, where your strength is renewed. Amazingly, God doesn't want us to visit the secret place; He wants us to dwell in the secret place. The Scripture says, *"He that dwelleth in the secret place of the Most High shall abide under the shadow of the Almighty."* (Psalm 91:1 [KJV]) Ever wonder why the instruction attached to the blessing was dwelling and not visiting? It's because of the benevolence act of God. He doesn't want you to walk out of His protection or cover; meanwhile, the moment you leave the secret place, you're prone to attacks that can mar or damage you.

In my book, *The Other Side of Grief*, I wrote that, "The secret place of the Most High is His presence, the place of fellowship. All those who have an active relationship with God are heirs of the promise above. So God is your refuge and fortress for you and your loved ones. You can be confident of this irrespective of past experiences. This is how you can be full of life and hope in a dark and dangerous world. You are not exposed to the elements like you think. Also, your life is not a candle in the wind waiting to be snuffed out."[27] A secret place is a place of fellowship; it's a place where you exchange your weakness and fears for strengths and faith.

If there is no secret place, then grief can thrive, but a secret place is where you are reassured of God's refuge. He is a refuge and a banner over you and your home, and this inadvertently blocks the whisperings and murmurings of the devil into your being. You can no longer hear his suggestions because the power and strength that flows from the secret place are profound and have equipped you for the next phase. Grief cannot stand the secret place; the secret place permits you to cry it out but fills you with excess joy thereafter.

Call to Action

- How will you start to renew your commitment to the secret place?

____

____

____

____

Prayer

Father, in the name of Jesus, I thank You for the understanding of the secret place. I pray that You help me to abide always in Your secret place. Help me to maintain my place before You at all times. I know I will find rest and peace in Your presence. I pray that You make me consistent with fellowship with You and the brethren. In Jesus' name. Amen.

Reflection

Day 25

FREE INDEED

Scriptural Text: *Christ has set us free! This means we are really free. Now hold on to your freedom and don't ever become slaves of the Law again.*

Galatians 5:1 (CEV)

Inspiring Commentary

Joy comes with freedom, especially when you're free from a factor that held you bound for quite some time. However, being free isn't enough; one must be free indeed. This means to be aware of your freedom and do things that aid the sustenance of such status. God isn't a taskmaster interested in freeing you today and putting you in bondage tomorrow. It saddens His heart to see that the one He died for is in bondage. The Scripture says, *"If the Son, therefore, shall make you free, ye shall be free indeed."* (John 8:36 [KJV])

In my book, *The Other Side of Grief,* I share that, "Having been set free from the shackles of grief, what next?... Your grief might have caused you to think you can't achieve, become or enjoy life as you should. You need to get rid of all that clutter and negative thinking. How? It depends on what you do with your freedom. First, having put your faith in God in your time of grief, you must believe with all your heart that God has set you free from the cloud of darkness that came with your grief. The devil is relentless and will want to get you back into the same old patterns. But you have to wear your freedom as a helmet of salvation and a shield of faith."[28] There is work that must be done on your part after freedom; there is decluttering that must take place. You must declutter from the residue of the feelings of bondage you found yourself in previous times. Because the devil might want to visit again with the same old patterns, but if you've been reconditioned, he'd understand that he is toiling with the wrong person.

Explore your freedom, be aware of its possibilities, and undergo a reconditioning that positions you for a courageous and fierce journey in Christ Jesus. Throw away shame because there is nothing to be ashamed of; you've been set free by the one in charge of liberty and freedom. What else? Study this freedom, know what it is and what it is not, and do not let naivety and ignorance get you into bondage once again.

Call to Action

- What are the areas you know you need to declutter?

____

____

____

____

Prayer

Father, in the name of Jesus, I thank You for Your sacrifice on Calvary for my sake. I pray that You engrave me to walk in the liberty you have made me free. I am no longer a slave to my grief or the situations I have been through. I pray that Your peace shall see me through this phase of my life. In Jesus' name. Amen.

Reflection

DAY 26

LIVING PURPOSEFULLY

Scriptural Text: *"Rejoice not against me, O mine enemy: when I fall, I shall arise; when I sit in darkness, the LORD shall be a light unto me.*

Micah 7:8 (KJV)

Inspiring Commentary

One of the potent weapons of grief in destroying a man is to place a veil of darkness upon the man not to see purpose in life. Unfortunately, this weapon has worked in different instances. You do not see any reason to live, you become slothful, and you exude apathy towards everything that comes your way. It's a plot from the devil, he sees what you cannot see, and he knows how glorious it is, so he's looking for tactics to evade you from accessing this reality. However, once freedom is gained, you must make it a maxim to live purposefully in and out of season. There's a purpose for your life, and since all things work together for your good, then the loss and pain must work together to achieve the purpose of which Christ has sent you into this world.

In my book, *The Other Side of Grief*, I expained that, "Grief has turned hardworking and successful people into sloths, scared to go to work. It's easy to adopt a habit of lazy-ing around and lying in bed all day during those days of mourning. But when that dark veil has been taken away and God has given you a new lease on life, you need to start living your life again."[29] Loss can be painful but shouldn't distract your attention from your purpose on earth. This is because if anything will be more painful, it is if, at the very end of it all, you still weren't able to accomplish your purpose. It will be much sadder than the loss.

You can't let life just happen; you must live according to God's standards and verdict. His instructions are your verdicts and stance, positioning you strategically for insurmountable growth and victory. Go to work, seek out that opportunity, learn that trade, run your business, and be preoccupied with the purpose you've been called to fulfill. When there is a lack of purpose, man lives life haphazardly, and sooner or later, the devil will find full expression in such a life and drown such an individual in the same place he was once taken from.

Call to Action

- Have you discovered your purpose in life, and how has grief kept you from pursuing it? If you need help discovering your purpose in life read my book, ***Fulfilling God's Purpose*** and the devotional.

____

____

____

____

Prayer

Father, in the name of Jesus, I thank You for not letting go of me. I pray that You will help me see my purpose despite the challenges around my life. I pray that You establish me on the path of Your purpose for my life. Every scale that has veiled me from Your purpose is destroyed in Jesus' name. I received a new fire in my spirit and a renewed passion for my assignment. In Jesus' name. Amen.

Reflection

DAY 27

THE ULTIMATE PANACEA

Scriptural Text: *"For the Word of God is quick, and powerful, and sharper than any two-edged sword, piercing even to the dividing asunder of soul and spirit, and of the joints and marrow, and is a discerner of the thoughts and intents of the heart."*

Hebrews 4:12 (KJV)

Inspiring Commentary

Panacea refers to something that has the power to cure every form of problem. Amazingly looking back and thinking about it, nothing created by man possesses this power to save but the Creator Himself. Only God created all things with the potency of having solutions to all things, and He machines this giant feat through His Word. The Scripture says, *"For the Word of God is quick, and powerful, and sharper than any two-edged sword, piercing even to the dividing asunder of soul and spirit, and of the joints and marrow, and is a discerner of the thoughts and intents of the heart." (*Hebrews 4:12) It has the efficacy of accessing and addressing every long-standing problem or new initiated ones. It is never caught unaware. On the other hand, ultimate refers to the greatest or the eventual, affirming that, after you've run shelter smelter without a solution, you will eventually come to the greatest panacea.

In my book, *The Other Side of Grief,* I wrote that, "God's Word is the ultimate panacea given by God over any situation. No matter what is happening around you or what you're going through, God is saying something. The quickness and power of His Word are demonstrated in that whatever your need is, His Word provides. Hence, when you find yourself in an undesirable situation, you're meant to search out in study and prayer what God is saying about that situation."[30] The Word of the Lord is the ultimate panacea; it possesses the power to revoke, rebuke and overcome grief.

The Scripture in (Isaiah 55:8-11 [MSG]) says, *"I don't think the way you think. The way you work isn't the way I work."* God's Decree. *"For as the sky soars high above earth, so the way I work surpasses the way you work, and the way I think is beyond the way you think. Just as rain and snow descend from the skies and don't go back until they've watered the earth, Doing their work of making things grow and blossom, producing seed for farmers and food for the hungry, So will the words that come out of my mouth not come back empty-handed. They'll do the work I sent them to do, they'll complete the assignment I gave them.* This affirms that the Word of the Lord does not only have the luxury of fulfilling what it set out to do. God's Word does not only have the power to heal sickness and the like; it also has the power to rebuke negative emotions that are eating deep into the human psyche. It's an all-around Word.

Call to Action

- What is your favorites Scripture that has kept you stable and consistent in your work with God?

____

____

____

____

Prayer

Father, in the name of Jesus, I thank You for the truth of Your Word. I pray that You keep me devoted to the truth of Your Word. I pray that You bind my heart to the instructions and dealings in Your Word. Let Your work remain a lamp to my feet, guiding me, lighting my paths out of misery into the fullness of joy. In Jesus' name. Amen.

Reflection

DAY 28

START LEARNING

Scriptural Text: *Repeat these basic essentials over and over to God's people. Warn them before God against pious nitpicking, which chips away at the faith. It just wears everyone out. Concentrate on doing your best for God, work you won't be ashamed of, laying out the truth plain and simple. Stay clear of pious talk that is only talk. Words are not mere words, you know. If they're not backed by a godly life, they accumulate as poison in the soul.*

2 Timothy 2:14-17a (MSG)

Inspiring Commentary

The presence of God within a man is usually cultivated. Just like a farmer cultivates the plant to yield substantive fruit and harvest, so also do you cultivate the presence of God. The presence of God shouldn't be learned until loss and pain happen. Although we do not cultivate the presence of God to avoid future loss or pain, it's part of the package. The presence of God does not possess a sole purpose, it's a box filled with several benefits, but you must not wait till the skies are blue before you make yourself an ally to the presence of God. Before the advent of loss or pain whatsoever, the presence of God must have taught you how to get over certain emotions and how to bask in His joy even when things don't look right. The lessons you've learned will come in handy at whatever point you need them; you wouldn't have to struggle with adapting to the lessons, which may seem weird, while still battling grief.

I explain in my book, *The Other Side of Grief* that, "It's vital to learn how to access and dwell in the presence of God. It is not when loss comes that you start learning to dwell in God's presence. It is something you should learn and apply to your daily living. You should acquire the ability to access and maintain God's presence throughout life's journey."[31] Start learning how to access the presence of God. For a man who has learned how to access the presence of God, not everything will throw you off balance because there is an understanding of the joy of the Lord being your strength.

Salvation is a prerequisite to learning the presence of God. You must first be saved; a Christian isn't taken aback by the happenings around him not because he doesn't see or hear them but because of his confidence in the One who saves him. Salvation opens us up to the joy that emanates from the presence of God, and this teaches our hearts to learn in little cases how not to slip when issues of life come along the way.

Call to Action

- Share below your experience being in God's presence since you got saved.

____

____

____

____

Prayer

Father, in the name of Jesus, I thank You for creating me in Your image. I pray that through the help of the Holy Spirit, You will teach me to learn Your presence. I pray that I will never be tired of Your presence or choose an alternative. I pray that You will help me enjoy the glory that radiates from Your presence. In Jesus' name. Amen.

Reflection

DAY 29

HOPE BEYOND THE GRAVE

Scriptural Text: *To whom God would make known what is the riches of the glory of this mystery among the Gentiles; which is Christ in you, the hope of glory:*

Colossians 1:27 (KJV)

Inspiring Commentary

The grave looks like the most terrible place as far as earth is concerned, and people don't like mentioning the word grave. It looks as though there is fear attributed to the term grave, but for Christians, we understand that there is hope beyond the grave. Our hope isn't only in temporary things that we can hold on to at the moment, but our hope is in eternity. The Scripture says, *"For we are saved by hope: but hope that is seen is not hope: for what a man seeth, why doth he yet hope for?"* Romans 8:24 The fact that it is not seen makes it hope, and the fact that it exists even beyond the grave makes it worthwhile.

In my book, *The Other Side of Grief*, I shared that, "As a believer, you must know that there is hope beyond the grave. Both for you and your loved ones. It's not the end of happiness in your life. The truth is that grief comes with a dark cloud of pain and bitterness that threatens your relationship with God and others. So you must learn how to maintain your fellowship with God and sustain your joy by seeing things through the lens of God's Word."[32] The Scripture says, *"If in this life only we have hope in Christ, we are of all men most miserable."* this shows us that, indeed, there is hope beyond the grave. Your hope isn't dashed after you lose a loved one; your faith and hope in Christ are stronger because you're sure that sooner or later, your hope will be made a reality.

The deep surge of losing a loved one can posit a dark cloud of pain, but you must find strength in the reality of the hope beyond the grave, which is not just in words but a reality that should gladden our hearts and dispel darkness. After Jesus died, on the third day, He rose in victory. Then rest assured that your loved one will rise on the last day, and you both will see each other, and this will be for eternity.

Call to Action

- What hope do you have in Christ despite the grief in your heart?

____

____

____

____

Prayer

Father, in the name of Jesus, I thank You for the hope I have found in Christ. When life was hopeless, everything fell apart. I thank You for the hope of salvation and eternal joy. I pray that You take away every sadness from my heart and keep me humbled in Your grace. I pray that You speak to my heart on the positivity and joy of knowing You. In Jesus' name. Amen.

Reflection

DAY 30

JOY IS ON THE WAY

Scriptural Text: *For His anger endureth but a moment; in His favor is life: weeping may endure for a night, but joy cometh in the morning.*

Psalm 30:5 (KJV)

Inspiring Commentary

It can be tiring while expecting or waiting for something or someone. However, while waiting for anything, one major force that can strengthen you is not just waiting for it passively but also waiting for it actively. Don't just wait for it; begin to live in it, begin to behave like it, take the position of having and possessing it already, whatsoever the thing might be. When you are not fully overwhelmed with joy, or you can't feel the presence of joy pervading through your being, start behaving as if you possess it already. Begin to bask in the euphoria, even when you're not necessarily feeling it; your emotions and feelings aren't the ones in charge; rather, your inner man is in charge. So, even when you're fully aware that joy hasn't submerged your being, intentionally provoke an upsurge of joy within your members in readiness for the real deal.

I shared these comforting insights in my book, *The Other Side of Grief,* "Just as the night doesn't last forever, the pain of losing a loved one can't last forever. You need to see this truth: your pain and sorrow will pass. You may not know how it'll come, but see your joy coming. God knows what you're going through, and He's not folding His arms. He's sending joy your way. Soon you'll have a reason to sing for joy and rejoice. All you need to do is hold on to God's Word."[33] See your joy coming, see grief been dislodged and dispelled, and view yourself as free from the verdicts and trap of the enemy.

Yes, grief is a natural response to the loss of a loved one, but it must not submerge you; you must not be lost in it; you must rise above grief and soak yourself in the joy of the Lord. This is because that is where comfort lies. No grieving person can access the joy of the Lord. Pray out of grief, praise your way out of it, cry your way of it, and then see your joy coming. Your world hasn't been shattered; God is bringing something notable out of that experience.

Call to Action

- What are the things that bring you joy?

____

____

____

____

- It's time to be deliberate about doing them. List a plan of action below.

____

____

____

____

Prayer

Father, in the name of Jesus, I thank You for the grace and truth I have experienced from Your Word. I pray that You fill my heart with Your joy. Let the river of joy flow ceaselessly through my heart. I bring my brokenness to You and pray that You mend them and fix my life. I walk and live in joy. In Jesus' name. Amen.

Reflection

ENDNOTES

1 Apostle L'Tanya C. Perry, MDiv., The Other Side of Grief (Charlotte, NC: TAP PRESS, 2023
2 Perry, MDiv.
3 Perry, MDiv.
4 16 inspirational quotes that will help you bounce back from 2020 - Inc.com. Accessed October 11, 2023. https://www.inc.com/maria-haggerty/16-inspirational-quotes-that-will-help-you-bounce-back-from-2020.html.
5 Perry, MDiv.
6 Perry, MDiv.
7 Perry, MDiv.
8 Perry, MDiv.
9 Perry, MDiv.
10 "A Quote from Peace Is Every Step." Goodreads. Accessed October 10, 2023. https://www.goodreads.com/quotes/124838-hope-is-important-because-it-can-make-the-present-moment.
11 Apostle L'Tanya C. Perry, MDiv., The Other Side of Grief (Charlotte, NC: TAP PRESS, 2023
12 Perry, MDiv.
13 Perry, MDiv.
14 Perry, MDiv.
15 Perry, MDiv.
16 Perry, MDiv.
17 Perry, MDiv.
18 Perry, MDiv.
19 Perry, MDiv.
20 Perry, MDiv.
21 Perry, MDiv.
22 Perry, MDiv.
23 Perry, MDiv.
24 Perry, MDiv.
25 Perry, MDiv.
26 Perry, MDiv.

27 Perry, MDiv.
28 Perry, MDiv.
29 Perry, MDiv.
30 Perry, MDiv.
31 Perry, MDiv.
32 Perry, MDiv.
33 Perry, MDiv.

Printed in the USA
CPSIA information can be obtained
at www.ICGtesting.com
LVHW021737171123
764239LV00007B/569

9 781957 052847